TADPOLE to FROG

Rachel Tonkin and Stephanie Fizer Coleman

WAYLAND
www.waylandbooks.co.uk

First published in Great Britain in 2019
by Wayland

Copyright © Hodder and Stoughton, 2019

Text first published in Looking at Lifecycles

All rights reserved

Editor: Melanie Palmer
Designer: Lisa Peacock

HB ISBN: 978 1 5263 1023 1
PB ISBN: 978 1 5263 1024 8

Printed and bound in China

Wayland, an imprint of
Hachette Children's Group
Part of Hodder and Stoughton
Carmelite House
50 Victoria Embankment
London EC4Y 0DZ
An Hachette UK Company
www.hachette.co.uk
www.hachettechildrens.co.uk

CONTENTS

Laying eggs	4	Mating	20
Inside the eggs	6	Frog life cycle	22
Hatching	8	Frog facts	24
Tadpole	10	Frog quiz	26
Back legs	12	Activities	28
Front legs	14	Frog words	31
Froglet	16	Index and answers	32
Adult frog	18		

Laying eggs

In spring, a female frog lays lots of eggs in a pond. The eggs are soft and stick together to make frogspawn.

Inside the eggs

The frogspawn floats to the top of the water. Inside each egg, a baby frog is growing. Each egg is kept safe in a ball of jelly.

Hatching

A baby frog is called a tadpole. After a few days the tadpole hatches out of its egg. It lives under the water.

Tadpole

The young tadpole breathes through gills on the side of its head. The tadpole eats tiny plants and small animals in the water.

Back legs

When the tadpole is about seven weeks old its back legs begin to grow. Its tail begins to shrink. Its gills are now tucked inside the skin.

Front legs

After nine weeks front legs grow. The tadpole now uses lungs inside its body to breathe. It comes to the surface of the water to get air.

Froglet

After 12 weeks the tadpole has become a young frog called a froglet. It can live on land and in water. Soon it will lose its tail altogether.

Adult frog

The froglet becomes an adult frog. It eats insects, worms and slugs to help it grow. In winter, the frog hibernates at the bottom of a pond.

Mating

In spring, the frog finds another frog to mate with. The female frog now lays lots of eggs of her own.

Frog facts

- Frogs lay between 3,000 and 4,000 eggs at any one time.

- Frogs do not need to drink as they take in water through their skin.

- Frogs' tongues are sticky to help them catch insects.

Frogs are very athletic – they can jump up to 20 times their own height.

Frogs do not just live near water. Some frogs live underground or even in trees.

Frog quiz

Test your new knowledge with this frog life cycle quiz by answering the questions below.

Question 1
What time of year do frogs lay eggs?

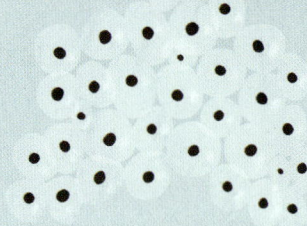

Question 2
What are frogs' eggs called?

Question 3
What are these?

Question 4
How does a tadpole breathe?

Question 5
How many legs has this tadpole got?

Question 6
How many legs has this tadpole got?

Question 7
This is a froglet. What has happened to the tadpole's tail as it changed into a froglet?

Question 8
How do frogs catch flies?

ANSWERS ON PAGE 32

Make a zigzag frog book

What you will need:
- Rectangle of thin card (the smaller the size, the smaller the book will be)
- Pens and pencils

1. Fold the card in half across its width.

2. Fold again, bending each end back on itself.

3. You now have a zigzag book.

4. Decide how you will fill it. You could record the different stages of a frog's life cycle, or fill it with facts and pictures of frogs, or frog words.

5. Don't forget to design a front cover!

Make a frog sock puppet

What you will need:
- Old sock • Googly eyes
- Fabric glue • Pencil
- Strip of red paper (about 7 cm long)

1. Find a clean old sock. Lots of frogs are green but some are yellow, red, orange, brown or blue so you decide what colour your frog will be.

2. Lay the sock on the table with the heel facing down. Flatten it out.

3. Use glue to stick the googly eyes at the bottom (toe end) of the sock.

4. Roll the strip of red paper around the pencil to make a rolled-up tongue.

5. Glue the end of the red paper where the frog's mouth will be.

6. Have fun making your frog puppet talk to people.

Tadpoles collage

What you will need:
- Paper plate
- Blue paint and paintbrush
- Scissors
- Black fabric
- Green wool
- Glue and spreader

1. Paint the paper plate blue. This is a pond for the tadpoles. Leave it to dry.

2. Cut out some tadpoles from black fabric. Stick them onto the pond.

3. Cut some lengths of green wool to make pondweed. Stick these to the pond.

4. Instead of fabric and wool, you could use paints to paint tadpoles and pondweed.

Frog words

Eggs
A baby frog grows inside an egg. Frogs' eggs are round.

Froglet
A tadpole becomes a froglet after 12 weeks.

Frogspawn
The eggs of a frog stick together. This is called frogspawn.

Gills
A tadpole has gills on the side of its head. It breathes through these under water.

Hibernate
To sleep through the winter.

Lungs
The organs in the chest which humans and many other animals use to breathe.

Mate
When a male and female frog make baby frogs.

Tadpole
A baby frog is called a tadpole. Tadpoles have long tails and live in water.

Index

breathe 10, 26, 31

eggs 4, 6, 8, 20, 22, 23, 24, 26, 31

froglet 16, 18, 23, 27, 31

frogspawn 4, 6, 22, 31

gills 10, 12, 22, 31

hatching 8, 22

lungs 14, 23, 31

mating 20, 23, 31

tadpole 8, 10, 12, 14, 16, 23, 31

water 6, 8, 10, 14, 16, 22, 23, 24, 25, 31

QUIZ ANSWERS: 1 Spring; **2** Frogspawn; **3** Tadpoles; **4** It uses gills to absorb oxygen from water; **5** Two back legs; **6** Four legs; **7** The froglet's tail has become very short. As a tadpole, its tail gradually gets smaller and smaller as it changes into a froglet, and then a frog; **8** Frogs shoot out their long, sticky tongue to catch flies.